# BOOK of STUPID MEN

I require only three things of a
man. He must be handsome,
ruthless and stupid.
– *Dorothy Parker*

# THE LITTLE BOOK
# OF STUPID MEN

Michael O'Mara Books Limited

First published in Great Britain in 1999 by
Michael O'Mara Books Limited
9 Lion Yard, Tremadoc Road, London SW4 7NQ

A CIP catalogue record for this book is available from the British Library

ISBN 1-85479-454-X

5 7 9 10 8 6 4

Edited by Alex Warren
Designed and typeset by Design 23
Printed and bound in England by William Clowes Ltd

What's the difference between
a stupid man and yoghurt?

*Yoghurt has culture.*

Why don't stupid men mind
their own business?

*No mind.*

What's the difference between a stupid man and a catfish?

*One's a bottom-feeding scum-sucker and the other is a fish.*

What's the difference between whales and stupid men?

*Whales mate for life.*

How are stupid men like commercials?

*You can't believe a word either one says and they both last about sixty seconds.*

Why did the stupid man put ice in his condom?

*To keep the swelling down.*

Why did the stupid man pour beer into his waterbed?

*He wanted a foam mattress.*

What did the experts of the nineties discover that could do the work of ten men?

*One woman.*

What do stupid men and beer bottles have in common?

*They're both empty from the neck up.*

Why are stupid men like laxatives?

*They both irritate the sh\*t out of you.*

How are stupid men like the weather?

*Nothing can be done to change either one of them.*

What do stupid men and decaffeinated coffee have in common?

*No active ingredients.*

How many stupid men does it
take to screw in a light bulb?

*Just one. They'll screw anything.*

How many stupid men does it
take to change a lightbulb?

*Ten, one to change the lightbulb,
and nine to congratulate him
down the pub.*

Why do stupid men name their penises?

*Because they want to be on a first name basis with the person who makes 95 per cent of their decisions.*

♂

What is a stupid man's idea of commitment?

*A second date.*

Why were men given larger
brains than dogs?

*So they wouldn't hump women's
legs at cocktail parties.*

Why did the stupid man buy a
new car?

*He couldn't keep up the
payments on the old one.*

Did you hear about the stupid guy who walked into a shop selling telephones?

*He bought a cordless phone for every room in the house.*

How do you make a stupid man take exercise?

*Hide the TV's remote control.*

What is a stupid man's idea
of foreplay?

*Half an hour of begging.*

What does a stupid man
think foreplay is?

*Something you do on a golf
course.*

How did the stupid man save a woman from being attacked?

*He controlled himself.*

What does a stupid man say when he finds his wife in bed with her lover?

*What are you doing?*

What's the difference between a stupid man and a yeti?

*One is covered with matted hair and stinks. The other lives on the top of a mountain.*

Why are stupid men like ghosts?

*They have to be seen to be believed.*

What does a stupid man say
before he picks his nose?

*Grace.*

Why is a stupid man modest?

*Because he has a lot to be
modest about.*

Why are stupid men happy?

*Because ignorance is bliss.*

Why do stupid men write
'T.G.I.F.' on their shoes?

*To remind them toes go in first.*

What's the difference between a stupid man and a monkey?

*A monkey can be trained to take out the garbage.*

Why is a stupid man like Santa Claus?

*Because he only comes once a year.*

What's the best way to a stupid man's heart?

*Who cares?*

What's the best way to get a stupid man to remember your anniversary?

*Get married on his birthday.*

How does a stupid man help with the housework?

*He lifts his legs as you vacuum.*

What is special about a stupid man's parachute?

*It opens on impact.*

How can you recognise a stupid man's helicopter?

*It has an ejection seat.*

Why did the stupid man go parachuting?

*Who knows why he does anything?*

How does a stupid man cook dinner?

*I don't know, he's never done it.*

What do men and dog poo have in common?

*The older they get the easier they are to pick up.*

What is the first prize in the
stupid man's lottery?

*£10 a year for a million years.*

What do people say when a
stupid man enters a room with
a beautiful woman on his arm?

*Where did you get that tattoo?*

How do stupid men define a
sharing relationship?

*They eat – we cook.*

Why is a stupid man like a
microwave?

*Thirty seconds and he's
finished.*

Why do men act stupid?

*Who says they're acting?*

What's the difference between
a stupid man and an
intelligent man?

*Nothing, they both think that
they know everything.*

Why doesn't a stupid man
believe in the new Messiah?

*Because to him a second
coming is an impossibility.*

Did you hear about the stupid
man who makes love like he
drives his car?

*He goes too fast and gets there
before anyone else.*

What do you call a stupid man who tidies up after himself?

*An over-achiever.*

What's the best way to keep a stupid man happy in the bedroom?

*Put the TV in the bedroom and turn on the football.*

How do you keep a stupid
man from wanting sex?

*Marry him.*

How do you know a fax is
from a stupid man?

*There's a stamp on it.*

How do you keep a stupid man
from wanting the other woman?

*Divorce him.*

What does a stupid man do
when confronted with a toddler
having a tantrum?

*Stamps his feet and shouts for
mother.*

What do you call a stupid man
who uses the rhythm method?

*Dad.*

How do we know that Adam
was a stupid man?

*Because he came first and they
all do.*

How do we know Adam was stupid?

*Would a clever man eat an apple when a naked woman was discussing temptation?*

Why was Adam a stupid man?

*He asked Eve if she was cheating on him.*

How is a stupid man like a
python?

*No sane person would go to
bed with either of them.*

How did the stupid man die
drinking milk?

*The cow fell on him.*

How many stupid men does it take to change the toilet roll?

*Don't know, it's never happened before.*

Why did the stupid man throw away his toilet brush?

*He discovered toilet paper.*

What's a stupid man's idea of a varied diet?

*A quarter-pounder with cheese one day, and without cheese the next.*

♂

Why don't stupid men's dogs do tricks?

*You have to be more intelligent than a dog to teach it tricks.*

Why did the stupid man buy
an electric lawnmower?

*So that he could find his way
back to the house.*

What's the difference between
a stupid man and a vibrator?

*A vibrator can't mow the lawn.*

How can you tell if a stupid man is cheating on you?

*He has a bath more than once a month.*

Why do stupid men drive BMW's?

*Because they can spell it.*

What's the difference between a stupid man and a shopping trolley?

*A shopping trolley has a mind of its own.*

♂

Why did the stupid man get a stabbing pain in his eye every time he drank a cup of tea?

*He forgot to take the spoon out.*

What do you call a stupid man with headphones on?

*Anything you like, he can't hear you.*

What do you see when you look into a stupid man's eyes?

*The back of his head.*

What's a stupid man's idea of safe sex?

*Masturbation.*

♂

What is a stupid man's view of safe sex?

*A padded headboard*

Why does a stupid man have a hole in his pocket?

*So he can count to six.*

What quality do most stupid men look for in a woman?

*Breathing.*

Did you hear about the stupid man who thought he was a half-breed?

*His father was a man and his mother was a woman.*

How does a stupid man make sex more interesting?

*He leaves town.*

Why did the stupid man lose
his job as a lift attendant?

*He couldn't learn the route.*

Did you hear about the stupid
newlywed who didn't know
the difference between putty
and Vaseline?

*His windows fell out.*

Why couldn't the stupid man
make ice cubes?

*He lost the recipe.*

Why did the stupid newly-
wed stay up all night?

*He was waiting for his sexual
relations.*

How are stupid men like carpet tiles?

*If you lay them properly the first time you can walk all over them for the rest of your life.*

Why does a stupid man only get half-hour lunch-breaks?

*So that his boss doesn't have to retrain him.*

How can you tell if a stupid man's cooked dinner?

*The salad's burnt.*

How does a stupid man know dinner is ready?

*The fire alarm goes off.*

How did the wife stop her
stupid husband biting his nails?

*She made him wear shoes.*

What is the best birth-control
device for a stupid man?

*His face.*

What's the useless piece of skin attached to the male member?

*A man.*

What does a stupid man say when he proposes marriage?

*You're going to have a what?*

Why did the stupid man put
his willy in boiling water?

*His wife told him to get*
*sterilised.*

How do you make a stupid
man's eyes twinkle?

*Shine a torch in his ear.*

How does a stupid man count money?

*1, 2, 3, 4, 5, another, another, another.*

There was a man so stupid he didn't know arson from incest.

*He set fire to his sister.*

How are stupid men like dogs?

*One stroke and they follow you everywhere.*

What happened when the stupid man phoned the sex chat-up line?

*The girl said: 'Not tonight, I've got earache.'*

What do you call ten stupid men in a circle?

*A dope ring.*

Did you hear about the stupid man who died at the height of passion?

*He came and went at the same time.*

My boyfriend's so stupid he
thinks that intercourse is a
racetrack.

♂

My boyfriend's so stupid he
thinks that Shirley Temple was
a children's synagogue.

My boyfriend's so stupid he thinks that *coq au vin* is sex in a truck.

My boyfriend's so stupid he thinks that *fellatio* is a character in Hamlet.

My boyfriend's so stupid he thinks that *genitalia* is the name of an Italian airline.

My boyfriend's so stupid he thinks a specimen is an Italian spacemen.

♂

My boyfriend's so stupid he thinks impotent means someone who's well known.

Why is a stupid man like old
age?

I: *Neither has many
advantages.*

II: *They both make women
depressed.*

III: *They both come too soon.*

Why does a stupid man like having two women in bed?

I: *So that he can come and go at the same time.*

II: *So that he can see double without having to buy a drink.*

III: *So that they have someone to talk to.*

What is a stupid man's idea
of safe sex?

I: *Not doing it on top of
scaffolding.*

II: *Doing it when his wife's
away.*

III: *Giving you a false name
and address.*

The stupid man's idea of a balanced diet is:

I: *Eating on one leg.*

II: *Leaving the crusts on his egg soldiers.*

III: *A six-pack in each hand.*

The stupid man thinks he's a wonderful lover because:

I: *He sends women into screaming fits.*

II: *He's faster than anyone else.*

III: *He practises a lot on his own.*

Why do stupid men think
that masturbation is better
than intercourse?

I. *Because they don't have to
buy flowers.*

II. *Because they don't have to
make conversation.*

III. *Because they don't have to
look their best.*

Why should you always be on top when you're in bed with a stupid man?

*Because they can only f\*\*k you up.*

♂

How are stupid men like Chinese meals?

*They satisfy you, but only for a little while.*

What's a stupid man's idea of foreplay?

*'You awake?'*

Why do stupid men enjoy fishing so much?

*Because it's the only time anyone says to them 'Wow! That's a big one!'*

A stupid man told his doctor
he could only achieve climax
in the doggy position.
'What's wrong with that?' said
the doctor.
'The dog's got bad breath.'

How are stupid men and
spray paint alike?

*One squeeze and they're all
over you.*

How does a stupid man get most of his exercise?

*By jumping to conclusions.*

How are stupid men like stamps?

*One lick and they'll stick to you.*

How are stupid men like
riding stables?

*They're both full of sh\*t.*

Why do stupid men like being
legless?

*It's the only time they can
boast that their willies touch
the floor.*

What's the difference between a stupid man and concrete?

*Concrete eventually gets hard.*

Which four-letter words offend stupid men?

*Don't and Stop.*

How are stupid men like
herpes?

*You can't get rid of either once
you've got them.*

What's the difference between
a stupid man and a condom?

*Condoms are no longer thick
and insensitive.*

What is a stupid man's idea
of oral contraception?

*Talking your way out of it.*

Why don't stupid men suffer
from haemorrhoids?

*Because they're such perfect
arseholes.*

What's a stupid man's idea of serious commitment?

'OK, I'll stay the night.'

How do you know when a stupid man's had an orgasm?

He snores.

What's the best use for a stupid man's bum?

*Parking your bike.*

How is a stupid man like the British economy?

*They're both in a terrible state.*

How is a stupid man like a set of car keys?

*Both are easily mislaid.*

How is a stupid man like the local council complaints office?

*Both are impossible to get through to when you need to talk.*

What won't a stupid man
stand for?

*A woman on the bus.*

How is a stupid man like an
old record?

*They both scratch a lot.*

What's a stupid man's idea of fairness in a relationship?

*Once with a condom on, once without.*

What does a stupid man think of circumcision?

*It's a rip off.*

How do you confuse a stupid man?

*You don't, they're born that way.*

Why does a stupid man talk about football?

*Because it would be boring to talk about tits all the time.*

What's a stupid man's idea of DIY?

*Making a cling-film condom.*

What do you get when you have two little balls in your hand?

*Your stupid man's undivided attention.*

What's the difference between a stupid man and a good book?

*You get pleasure out of a good book.*

How can you tell a stupid man at a wedding?

*He's the one kissing the rottweiler.*

What do you get if you cross a stupid man with a gorilla?

*A really stupid gorilla.*

♂

What's the difference between a stupid man and wine?

*Wine matures.*

Why do stupid men become
smarter during sex?

*Because they're plugged into a
genius.*

Why don't women have
stupid men's brains?

*Because they don't have
penises to put them in.*

Why did God make man before woman?

*She needed a rough draft before she made the final copy.*

Why is a stupid man's pee yellow and his sperm white?

*So he can tell if he's coming or going.*

Why are blonde jokes so short?

*So that stupid men can remember them.*

How can you tell if a stupid man is sexually excited?

*He's breathing.*

How do you scare off a stupid
man?

*Tell him you love him and
you want his children.*

How do you save a stupid
man from drowning?

*Take your foot off his head.*

Why do gentlemen prefer
blondes?

*They like people of their own
intellectual ability.*

What do you call a man with
an IQ of 50?

*Gifted.*

Why do men always have
stupid looks on their faces?

*Because they are stupid.*

How do stupid men sort out
their laundry?

*Filthy, and filthy but wearable.*

What's the difference between a stupid man and ET?

*ET phoned home.*

Why is psychoanalysis quicker for stupid men than for women?

*Because when it's time to go back to his childhood, he's already there.*

What is a stupid man's most effective contraceptive?

*His personality.*

How many stupid men does it take to tile a bathroom?

*It depends how thinly you slice them.*

Did you hear about the stupid man who went to the luggage shop and asked for seven overnight bags?

*He was going away for a week.*

What's the difference between a pig and a stupid man?

*There are some things even a pig won't do.*

Why do stupid men's hearts
make the best transplants?

*They've never been used.*

How do you make a stupid
man laugh on Monday?

*Tell him a joke on Friday.*

How are stupid men like blenders?

*You know you need one, but you're not quite sure why.*

A stupid man was trying to chat up an attractive woman in a bar and used his best line: 'Haven't I seen you somewhere before?' 'Yes,' she replied. 'I'm the receptionist at the VD clinic.'

What do you call an intelligent man in England?

*A tourist.*

Why are stupid men like chocolates?

*They never last long enough.*

How do stupid men exercise
on the beach?

*They suck in their stomachs
when they see a bikini.*

What do you do when your
stupid boyfriend walks out?

*Shut the door.*

Why is it dangerous to let a
stupid man's mind wander?

*It's too little to be allowed out
on it's own.*

What do you do if your best
friend runs off with your
stupid husband?

*You miss her dreadfully.*

What is the difference between a stupid man and giving birth?

*One is painful, almost unbearable, whilst the other is just having a baby.*

What do you call a stupid man wearing handcuffs?

*Trustworthy.*

Why are stupid men like lawnmowers?

*They're hard to get started, emit foul smells and don't work half the time.*

Why should you never hit a stupid man with glasses?

*Because you should hit him with a brick instead.*

Other "Little Book" titles published by
Michael O'Mara Books Ltd:

The Little Book of Farting – ISBN 1-85479-445-0

The Little Book of Venom – ISBN 1-85479-446-9

The Little Toilet Book – ISBN 1-85479-456-6

The Little Book of Pants – ISBN 1-85479-477-9

If you would like more information, please contact
our UK Sales Department: Fax: 020 7 622 6956
E-mail: jokes@michaelomarabooks.com